PRODUCTIVITY FOR SCHOOL BUSINESS PROFESSIONALS

COMPANION WORKBOOK

JULIE CORDINER

SCHOOL FINANCIAL SUCCESS PUBLICATIONS

Productivity for School Business Professionals Companion Workbook

Published by School Financial Success Publications

https://schoolfinancialsuccess.com

Cover design: JD Smith

ISBN: 978-0-9955902-4-3

Table of Contents

Your Productivity Workbook

Purpose

This workbook is a companion to the main book, 'Productivity for School Business Professionals'; it is not a substitute for it. You can use it as a journal to explore your thoughts and ideas about the areas you want to change as you work through the activities in the main book.

I hope it will also provide a helpful record of your starting point and encourage you to reflect on all the questions and prompts in each activity. As I explain in the book, writing by hand allows you to think deeply and let your creativity emerge. You will be able to identify solutions, understand your emotions and motivation, and make better decisions.

Content

The workbook includes a very brief summary of the background to each activity, but you should refer to the narrative in the main book to fully appreciate the context and see how each one fits within the overall improvement plan. This will help you complete the activities in a more meaningful way.

For some of the activities, you'll find extra prompts which don't appear in the book. I hope these are helpful, but they are not meant to limit you. Try to think of further questions appropriate to your situation as an individual and in relation to your post and the school you're working in.

The pages are blank rather than lined, to allow you full expression; you may prefer to draw diagrams or doodle; use it in whatever way appeals to you. I have provided additional pages at the back in case you need more space.

Activity 1: Your Starting Point

Chapter 2: A system for change

This activity sets a baseline for your whole productivity journey, so you can look back at it and measure the progress you've made after completing all the activities.

1.1   Find a quiet time and place. Write about the position you are starting from. Express your feelings about the situation you're in and the way you approach your work and your personal life.

For it to be helpful as a baseline, be honest, go deep, and recognise the positive and negative aspects. Try to identify the big things you'd like to change. It needs to be personal to you.

Prompts:

- What is your dominant feeling? Is this typical, long-standing, or fairly recent? Can you pinpoint why you feel this way?
- Which personal and professional challenges do you relish and cope with easily?
- What pressures do you find difficult, both personally and professionally?
- How do you handle these challenges and pressures?
- Do your approaches differ for positive and negative situations?
- How would you score your current productivity levels on a scale of 1 (terrible, never get anything done) to 10 (fully efficient and achieving my goals effortlessly)?
- Why have you decided on that score?
- What are the barriers that prevent you from being more efficient?
- What would you most like to change?

1.2   Reflect on what you've written (after an interval if you can) and add any new thoughts that have occurred to you.

Activity 1: Your Starting Point

Activity 1: Your Starting Point

Activity 1: Your Starting Point

Activity 2: Time Tracking

Chapter 2: A system for change

Understanding how you spend your time now is an invaluable first step. It will highlight obvious areas where you're less efficient and can achieve quick wins. Initially, you're only going to do the exercise; there is a separate activity later in the book to analyse the results. This is an exercise you can repeat from time to time to sharpen your time management.

2.1   Download a time tracking spreadsheet template from the links webpage at https://schoolfinancialsuccess.com/psbp-links.

2.2   Choose a fairly typical week (I know there's no such thing, but just pick one). At regular intervals, record your activity in the relevant time blocks in your worksheet. Create bigger blocks if needed, using the Merge Cells function. Try to record a full week; mixing days from different weeks won't give you a complete picture. If you can do two weeks, copy the sheet to a new tab.

2.3   Add useful notes (either on the sheet or in here) about things that weren't typical, any specific challenges or deadlines you were working to, or any other information which will be helpful when you look back at it.

Tips for completing the activity can be found in the first tab within the file.

It's important to carry out the instructions, then save the file and keep it safe while you read on. We will be coming back to it later; don't try to analyse the results now.

Activity 2: Time Tracking

Activity 3: Negative beliefs

Chapter 3: Mindset

To avoid self-sabotage, it's important to challenge your own assumptions as the first step in addressing internal barriers to productivity. We'll start with negative beliefs.

3.1 Make a list of any negative beliefs you hold. They can be from any part of your life. Are they self-sabotaging?

3.2 Write about why you believe each one. How does it make you feel? Does it limit you in any way?

Reflection

Did you come up with many negative beliefs? Did any of them surprise you?

For each one, write a note about an occasion when you were given evidence which contradicts it: an event, situation or conversation which showed you performed well or were appreciated.

For each contradictory example, how did it make you feel? Can you recognise and accept the positive evidence? For some reason we're often reluctant to give ourselves credit. Well, I'm giving you permission to do exactly that, in case you need it.

You should now be able to cross off some of the unhelpful beliefs, or at least know you can address them. This is a simple but effective way of changing your perceptions of yourself, which is a key ingredient of your mindset.

Activity 3: Negative beliefs

Activity 3: Negative beliefs

Activity 3: Negative beliefs

Activity 4: Positive beliefs

Chapter 3: Mindset

This activity helps you reinforce your positive assumptions as a way of battling against the negative ones and encourages you to think about the overall balance between the two.

4.1   Write a list of positive beliefs you hold about yourself.

4.2   For each one, write about why you believe it. How does it make you feel? Can you think of a time when it gave you the confidence to try something new, or approach something in a different way?

Affirmations like this are powerful, so if you have identified a positive belief which is linked to an important goal, write it on a piece of card and keep it somewhere handy to look at when you're in need of a boost.

Reflection

Consider your lists from activities 3 and 4. What's the overall balance between the two? Are there more positive or negative beliefs? Can you come up with any other ways to tackle the remaining negative beliefs and reinforce the positive ones?

If you are having a hard time over something, look back at your notes from this activity. Focus on the positive beliefs first, then your contradictory evidence on the negative beliefs. You can add more or repeat the exercise if it helps.

Activity 4: Positive beliefs

Activity 4: Positive beliefs

Activity 4: Positive beliefs

Activity 5: Handling pressure

Chapter 4: Self-care

For strong mental and emotional health, you need to minimise stress. This activity helps you to identify the main causes of it and use the tips in chapter 4 to tackle them.

5.1 Make a list of the situations which cause you to feel under pressure, at work or at home. Do they have anything in common? Can you work out any ways of preventing them?

5.2 Now think about how you handle the situations on your list. Could you do things differently next time? How? What sources of support might be available to you?

5.3 What healthy habits can you develop, to increase your resilience and enable you to bounce back from difficult times?

Activity 5: Handling pressure

Activity 5: Handling pressure

Activity 5: Handling pressure

Activity 6: What energises you?

Chapter 5: Know Yourself

We need to maintain high energy to motivate ourselves for productive work. Notice what energises you so you can take opportunities to create the feeling more often.

6.1   Take a few minutes to make a list of the people and/or things which energise you.

6.2. Can you identify why they have this effect?

6.3. Can you put into words how they make you feel?

Reflection

Now do some writing about how you could make more space for the people and pursuits you've listed, and whether there are any other activities which would have the same effect. Keep this list in mind when you are building your goals in the next chapter.

Activity 6: What energises you?

Activity 6: What energises you?

Activity 6: What energises you?

Activity 7: What drains you?

Chapter 5: Know Yourself

Many things can be draining - complex or boring work, pointless meetings, and people. If you understand which of them drain your energy, you can be watchful and minimise them.

7.1   Make a list of people, tasks and anything else which drains you.

7.2   How do they make you feel?

7.3   Why do they have this effect?

7.4   What could you do about it?

Activity 7: What drains you?

Activity 7: What drains you?

Activity 7: What drains you?

Activity 8: Analysing habits

Chapter 6: Habits

Habits can creep up on us, so it's good to spot them and know if they are constructive or destructive so we can re-balance them. Read chapter 6 carefully to help you with this activity.

8.1 Make two lists of habits: ones which help you to be efficient and effective, and those that are holding you back.

8.2 How did you create the positive habits? Was it a conscious decision, and if so, how did you go about it?

8.3 Decide which negative habits you need to change. Jot down some ideas on how to stop them or replace them with helpful habits.

Prompts:

- Can you change the cue, routine or reward?
- How could you use the Four Laws of Behaviour Change and habit stacking to make it easier?

Activity 8: Analysing habits

Activity 8: Analysing habits

Activity 8: Analysing habits

Activity 9: What is your 'Why'?

Chapter 9: Goal setting

To create meaningful goals, you need to understand your deep-seated internal reasons for wanting to do well in this job. It will remind you why you chose it when things get tough.

9.1   Write for at least ten minutes about why you do what you do.

9.2   Think of all the people, events and situations which have shaped your decisions.

Prompts:

- What is it about your nature, your aptitude and abilities, that make this career a good fit for you?
- What attracted you to your current job?
- What led to your choice of this school or previous places where you were given opportunities to grow your skills?

9.3   Find the best statement among your writing which sums up your 'Why', and make a poster out of it, either by hand or using the free tool at Canva.com to create a background image and attractive text. Stick it on your wall; when things get difficult, you'll have a visual reminder of why you're doing all this.

Activity 9: What is your 'Why'?

Activity 9: What is your 'Why'?

Activity 9: What is your 'Why'?

Activity 10: Who do you want to be?

Chapter 7: Goal setting

Understanding who you want to be will make your goals purposeful, motivating you to achieve them. You will have a clear pathway at the core of your productivity plan and your progress will be more rewarding.

10.1   Jot down your thoughts on what sort of person you want to be, and what success would mean to you.

Prompts:

- Which aspects of your job do you most enjoy, where you can make a real difference?
- Describe your feelings when something goes well.
- If you left this job, what would you like your boss to say about you at your leaving presentation?
- What would you like to move on to next (it could be something totally different)?
- What do you envisage your long-term career might look like?
- Would you like your personal life to be different in some way? How?

Activity 10: Who do you want to be?

Activity 10: Who do you want to be?

Activity 10: Who do you want to be?

Activity 11: Your strategic goals

Chapter 7: Goal setting

Strategic goals are ambitious and inspiring, the big ideas that will drive all your efforts. So it's worth taking time to identify what yours are across all parts of your life.

You'll be using your notes from activities 9 and 10 in this exercise, and you'll also need a pack of sticky notes.

11.1 Scribble down any big goals which come to mind, both personal and professional, one per sticky note.

11.2 Check they will take you closer to who you want to be, and that they are consistent with your purpose, your 'Why'.

11.3 Try to imagine yourself in five or even ten years' time. What could be different if you achieve your goals?

11.4 Keep the sticky notes, as you'll need them for a future activity.

The possibilities are endless, limited only by your imagination, so find a place where you can relax and let your subconscious mind bring up ideas. Free writing is effective for this sort of exercise.

Reflection

When you've run out of ideas, stand back and look at them. How different are they from any you've set in the past? What does this suggest about your future potential?

Now look for any themes. Are some of them similar in intent? Group them together. Write down your list of goals here; we'll be returning to them soon.

Activity 11: Your strategic goals

Activity 12: Review of work-related goals

Chapter 7: Goal setting

It's worth making sure your work-related goals are targeted to the school's vision and aims and that they are deliverable, otherwise you'll be wasting your valuable time. Use your results to check with your manager that you are focusing on things which will make a difference to the school.

12.1   Consider the list you compiled in Activity 11 and put a mark against any which have to be there because of your current job. Add any big goals you have missed.

12.2   Ask yourself a series of questions to check if they're appropriate and deliverable.

Prompts:

- Are they the right goals to deliver what the organisation needs?
- Do you have a fair chance of achieving them?
- Are the timescales realistic, given the work involved?
- What measures will be used to assess your progress and achievement?
- Are your success measures relevant, transparent, fair and easily quantified?

12.3   Record your thoughts below.

Reflection

Look at your notes. Has this review of your proposed goals unearthed any problems? Has it highlighted any reasons why you're struggling to be productive or show impact in what you're doing?

Activity 12: Review of work-related goals

Activity 12: Review of work-related goals

Activity 12: Review of work-related goals

Activity 13: Prioritise your goals

Chapter 7: Goal setting

You need to keep your most important goals firmly in mind as you schedule your work, so knowing their priority order is important. After doing this activity, they'll be crystal clear.

13.1   Return to your sticky notes from Activity 11.

13.2   Arrange the notes in a pyramid shape, with one at the top level, two at the next, then three, four and so on. Place those which matter most to you at the top, then work across and down. They're all important, so think about the relativity between them. Use the prompts below and jot down your reasons/comments in here.

13.3   Play with them until you're happy with the order; you might suddenly realise one of them is a burning desire.

13.4   If you have more than three rows, remove those below the third row and put them to one side. Double check the six remaining items; these are your top priorities. Some of the discarded items (medium-sized rocks and pebbles) can still be fitted in with good organisation but the top six are the vital ones.

13.5   Take a photo or draw the pyramid in here to record it for future reference.

Prompts for step 13.2:

- Which of your goals will most help you realise your dreams?
- Which will set the foundation for significant benefits in the future?
- If you could only do one thing, which would it be? If you could only do two, what would you add? If three, what would be the third?
- Ask others for their view; they will have a different perspective and could help you see things in a fresh way.

Reflection

What do your choices mean for the new balance you're trying to create? What will you be doing differently if you follow this path? Will it feel right?

Do you need to give up any of the discarded items? How different will you feel if you do?

Activity 13: Prioritise your goals

Activity 13: Prioritise your goals

Activity 13: Prioritise your goals

Activity 14: Break down your priority goals

Chapter 8: From goals to a plan

Break down your priority goals to make them more manageable and less scary.

Find a quiet place. You'll need a flip chart pad, a pen and sticky notes in several colours.

14.1   Write the first priority goal from Activity 13 on a sticky note and put it at the centre of a piece of flip chart paper.

14.2   Write down each step you need to take to achieve it, one per sticky note, and add them to the paper. Summarise large projects in a few sticky notes; you can divide them up later.

14.3   Work quickly and let the ideas flow. Don't stop and don't judge; just write down whatever emerges.

14.4   Repeat for the other priority goals in different colours on individual pages.

14.5   Consult your current To Do list for any extra items.

14.6   Take a photo of your final results for future reference.

14.7   Create a planning document and transfer the steps into it, arranging them under each goal in a logical order with a clear description. This will form the start of your new work plan. Keep the sticky notes; you'll be re-using them soon.

Reflection

Review the steps under each priority goal in your planning document. Do you need to rearrange any of the items, group them differently or change the sequence?

Add helpful notes here for developing the plan further. You could sketch out the parts of a project, plot inter-dependencies or work out a sequence.

See https://schoolfinancialsuccess.com/psbp-links for an example of the sticky note activity, based on my planning for an online course 'Developing an Income Generation Strategy'.

Activity 14: Break down your priority goals

Activity 14: Break down your priority goals

Activity 14: Break down your priority goals

Activity 15: Your important/urgent matrix

Chapter 8: From goals to a plan

Work out which tasks only you can do, so you don't waste your time on unnecessary items.

15.1 Create an Important/Urgent matrix on a large sheet of paper and plot the sticky notes from Activity 14 on it. You might need to break down some of them into individual notes if they fall into different quadrants. Think about the relative importance and urgency of each item to the rest.

15.2 Review the chart and move the sticky notes around until you're happy with the results.

15.3 In your planning document, mark the quadrant number against each of the items in a separate column. This will allow you to sort them by quadrant number if desired.

15.4 For items in quadrant 4, either remove them from your planning document or add the necessary action to allow you to eliminate them.

Most of this exercise is done outside the workbook, but you can make notes below to record reasons for your decisions or comment on the relative importance of items.

Activity 15: Your important/urgent matrix

Activity 16: Your planning system

Chapter 8: From goals to a plan

Keep your goals and tasks visible through a clear and comprehensive planning system, so you can easily keep on top of duties and deadlines.

16.1 Write some notes on how you currently record your goals and track your progress. What works for you, and are there any aspects which aren't as effective? Does it help you schedule tasks at the right times, ensure nothing is missed, and motivate you? How could your system be improved?

16.2 Decide what combination of systems you will use in the future. Record here what you intend to do and how it will make you more productive.

16.3 Test out your ideas for a trial period.

16.4 After your trial, come back to this activity, re-read your notes and decide whether you've achieved what you intended. Make some notes on how it went; tweak it for another trial period if needed.

Activity 16: Your planning system

Activity 16: Your planning system

Activity 16: Your planning system

Activity 17: Choose your shortcuts

Chapter 9: Be organised

Achieve a balance between your priority goals and all the unknown demands that come flooding in on a daily basis, by capturing your commitments. Use shortcuts to get the important things done, using the information, tools and techniques in chapter 9.

17.1   Review the information in chapter 9 and make notes on how you can better organise your work.

17.2   Create a list of techniques and shortcuts to save time.

17.3   Make time to trial a selection over the next month.

17.4   At the end of the month, return to these notes and record your findings.

17.5   Repeat with another set until you find the right balance.

Activity 17: Choose your shortcuts

Activity 17: Choose your shortcuts

Activity 17: Choose your shortcuts

Activity 18: What could you have refused?

Chapter 10: Set boundaries

Learn to limit the demands placed on you by saying no to non-essential requests from people who can do it themselves. Be prepared by doing some thinking in advance about how you can respond.

18.1   Look back over the last couple of months and make a list of the things outside your remit which you didn't want to do but ended up doing anyway.

18.2   Make some notes here about each situation: your feelings at the time, and how you could have handled it differently. Could you have said no to anything? What would have been the consequences, for them and for you?

18.3   If you think refusal would have damaged your relationship with the person, are you sure? Does it hinge on their expectation that you'll drop everything and run to their assistance? Consider the boundaries and dynamics of the relationship. Most things can be handled with understanding on both sides.

Activity 18: What could you have refused?

Activity 18: What could you have refused?

Activity 18: What could you have refused?

Activity 19: Your 'saying no' phrases

Chapter 10: Set boundaries

Think of some phrases to use when you want to say no to unnecessary and unimportant work. It will make it far easier to refuse requests.

19.1   Use your examples from the last activity to construct some 'No' phrases to use in similar situations in the future.

19.2   Visualise yourself saying them to someone you know. Practise, so you can speak confidently if an occasion arises.

Activity 19: Your 'saying no' phrases

Activity 20: Delay, delegate, eliminate

Chapter 10: Set boundaries

Give some careful thought to how you can handle the items in quadrants 2, 3 and 4 from your Eisenhower Matrix. Preparation will help you to make the right decisions and banish overwhelm.

20.1 Consider your routine tasks and processes. Identify a series of questions to expose potential eliminations or adjustments and list them here.

Prompts:
- Are the tasks still needed?
- Are they effective?
- What do they achieve?
- What would happen if you stopped doing them, lengthened the timescales, did them less frequently or performed them to a lower standard?

20.2 Use the advice in chapter 10 to add appropriate actions to your planning document for the items on your list.

20.3 Look at all the quadrant 2, 3 and 4 actions in your planning document and check you have the right actions and timescales for delaying, delegating and eliminating as required.

Activity 20: Delay, delegate, eliminate

Activity 20: Delay, delegate, eliminate

Activity 20: Delay, delegate, eliminate

Activity 21: Managing expectations

Chapter 10: Set boundaries

Analyse information from your time tracking and planners to check your workload and manage expectations, both what others expect of you and what you expect of members of your team.

21.1 Use all available sources to make an honest assessment of whether the demands on you are reasonable or not.

21.2 Do some free writing about how you can tackle the situation, and act on it, e.g. gathering evidence to discuss with your manager, or finding ways to increase your efficiency.

21.3 Make notes on how you convey your expectations to staff. Think up some ideas using the advice in this chapter.

21.4 Where appropriate, build actions into your planning document.

Activity 21: Managing expectations

Activity 21: Managing expectations

Activity 21: Managing expectations

Activity 22: Time tracking reflections

Chapter 11: Time management

Now's the time to analyse your time tracking results and spot areas for improvement. Be honest and pay careful attention to what you need to change.

22.1 Return to your initial time tracker and analyse the results to detect any patterns. Ask yourself some questions along the lines I've suggested above, to identify your main areas of inefficiency. Make notes on them here.

22.2 How could you spend your day more productively? Do some free writing about what you need to change and how to approach it.

22.3 Turn these into actions and schedule them or put reminders in an appropriate place for behavioural changes.

Activity 22: Time tracking reflections

Activity 22: Time tracking reflections

Activity 22: Time tracking reflections

Activity 23: Tackling interruptions

Chapter 11: Time management

Interruptions can play havoc with your concentration and stop you achieving your goals, so work out a plan to change how you react and protect your time.

23.1 Using the evidence from your tracker and your own instincts, list in your workbook the most common and significant interruptions you face.

23.2 Refer to the tips in this section and identify the actions you plan to take to limit these interruptions.

Activity 23: Tackling interruptions

Activity 23: Tackling interruptions

Activity 23: Tackling interruptions

Activity 24: Mastering email

Chapter 11: Time management

The two areas to get a grip of are clearing a backlog of emails and finding a system to keep on top of ongoing emails. It will be even better if you can do it across all teams in school.

24.1   Jot down your plans for tackling the backlog of emails and keeping on top of new ones from this point onwards.

24.2   Arrange an agenda item at your next team meeting to get ideas for a new approach to managing emails.

Activity 24: Mastering email

Activity 24: Mastering email

Activity 24: Mastering email

Activity 25: Set the conditions for flow

Chapter 12 Achieve flow

You need to cultivate a flow state for maximum concentration, where the work feels effortless. Chapter 12 outlines several ways to achieve this; experiment to find out what is most effective.

25.1 Write about the following:
- What conditions will help you get into a flow state for longer periods?
- How could you create these conditions? Which techniques are you going to try?
- How will this make a difference to your productivity, i.e. both the quantity and quality of your work?

25.2 Set a trial period of at least a month, and test out your new techniques.

25.3 At the end of the trial, return to this activity and make notes on what happened. Tweak and try again until you find what is best for you.

Activity 25: Set the conditions for flow

Activity 25: Set the conditions for flow

Activity 25: Set the conditions for flow

Activity 26: Understanding procrastination

Chapter 13: Tackle resistance

Resistance stops you making progress; a common response to it is procrastination, the art of delaying things which you could easily and quickly do now. Understanding what this looks like for you will help you to realise how damaging it is to your level of productivity.

26.1   Answer these questions to understand what procrastination means for you:
- What are you trying to avoid when you procrastinate?
- What has your procrastination cost you in the past?
- What will it cost you in the future if you don't tackle it?
- If the thing you're procrastinating over suddenly became easy, what would it mean for you, your colleagues, friends and/or family? What would you gain? How would it feel?

Activity 26: Understanding procrastination

Activity 26: Understanding procrastination

Activity 26: Understanding procrastination

Activity 27: Plan to beat resistance

Chapter 13: Tackle resistance

It's time to get specific about what you are resisting doing and make plans to tackle it instead of procrastinating, using the suggestions in the chapter.

27.1 List the most significant examples of work you regularly resist.

27.2 For each one, consider the five-point plan in the 'Beat resistance' section of the book and note down any strategies you believe would be effective in making you do the tasks sooner.

27.3 If you struggle, refer back to your writing for activity 26 on the impact of procrastination, to remind yourself of why you need to address the delayed tasks.

Activity 27: Plan to beat resistance

Activity 27: Plan to beat resistance

Activity 27: Plan to beat resistance

Activity 28: Stay Fix opportunities

Chapter 14: Build capacity

You can save a lot of time by tackling underlying problems instead of answering the same questions repeatedly or correcting system issues over and over again. Identify any similar issues that you are facing, find the source for each and create a plan to address it.

28.1   Identify any problems which could be solved with a Stay Fix approach. For each one, what's the underlying issue you need to address?

28.2   Write down your thoughts about an initial set of steps you can take to achieve a long-term solution.

Activity 28: Stay Fix opportunities

Activity 28: Stay Fix opportunities

Activity 28: Stay Fix opportunities

Activity 29: Self-service opportunities

Chapter 14: Build capacity

Getting your community (parents, staff, pupils, governors) to help themselves can free up a lot of time which you and your staff can make better use of. Think broadly and creatively.

29.1 Review the self-service systems you currently operate and identify opportunities you haven't yet taken advantage of.

29.2 Find people to test parent-focused information on your website. Act on the feedback and discuss potential improvements with your website coordinator.

29.3 Check existing systems to see if you already have the facility to introduce new self-service processes.

29.4 Ask other SBPs in local or national networks for advice on what's been successful for them.

29.5 Prepare a cost-benefit analysis of the cost of a new system or additional module, compared to the savings in staff time and any other associated expenditure.

29.6 Assess the risks in your proposals, then discuss the options for change with your SLT.

Activity 29: Self-service opportunities

Activity 29: Self-service opportunities

Activity 29: Self-service opportunities

Activity 30: Lessons from change

Chapter 14: Build capacity

If you are proactive and communicate well when leading change, it will smooth the way and you won't spend as much time on conflict resolution or tackling reluctant staff. One way to prepare is to think about lessons learned from your past experience of change.

30.1   Reflect on a previous change you've led and do some writing in your workbook on the lessons you learned.

Prompts:

- How did you engage others to get their cooperation?
- Did you involve them early enough?
- Were your methods of communication effective?
- Did you need to take any corrective action to get the plans back on track?
- What other lessons did you learn?
- What will you do differently next time you lead change?

Activity 30: Lessons from change

Activity 30: Lessons from change

Activity 30: Lessons from change

Activity 31: Assess your skills

Chapter 15: Hone your skills

Reviewing your skills and deciding where to focus your future development will help you direct your time effectively. Keep an eye on what you need for your next career move.

31.1 Make an honest (re-)assessment of your aptitudes and skills. What are your strongest areas and training needs?

31.2 Read your reflections on 'Who do you want to be?' (Activity 10). Are there other areas you want to develop?

31.3 Group your training needs under priority goal headings and use them in your next appraisal.

Activity 31: Assess your skills

Activity 31: Assess your skills

Activity 31: Assess your skills

Activity 32: Should I stay or go?

Chapter 16: The culture around you

Being in a job that is incompatible with your beliefs and needs can diminish your productivity and make you unhappy. You need to think carefully about whether this is the right place for you before committing a lot of effort to making improvements.

32.1   If you're not sure whether this is the job for you, do some free writing to try to understand your feelings.

Prompts:

- What are the positive things about your situation?
- What makes you uncomfortable? Is it one problem or several? Can you pinpoint why it's making you feel this way?
- Is the situation causing problems for you in other respects besides at work?
- Can you imagine being able to resolve it?

Activity 32: Should I stay or go?

Activity 32: Should I stay or go?

Activity 32: Should I stay or go?

Activity 33: Scope for change

Chapter 16: The culture around you

Before rushing into a decision about moving somewhere else, it's wise to give your existing job and school a chance. Get your head straight and systematically work through what might or might not be possible.

33.1 List the aspects of your role which you dislike but which could be improved in some way. Flag them as crucial, desirable or optional. Desirable means they would make a real difference, but you can put up with them if they can't be changed. Optional items are little niggles, nice to change but probably not worth the effort.

33.2 List the areas where you're highly productive or have the chance to be. Flag them as crucial, desirable or optional.

33.3 Make a wish list of changes which would enable you to achieve maximum productivity. Flag them as before.

33.4 The list in 33.2 is your benchmark for what motivates you. Set this 'List 2' aside for now; you'll come back to it later.

33.5 Consider the 'crucial' elements to improve in lists 1 and 3. Write down ideas for change to help you stay in this job.

33.6 How easy or difficult will it be to implement each change? How long might it take, and are you willing to wait?

33.7 If your answers suggest it's worth a try, develop a plan to make the changes happen.

Activity 33: Scope for change

Activity 33: Scope for change

Activity 33: Scope for change

Activity 34: Your productivity action plan

Chapter 17: Making the changes

You will have lots of ideas for changes that you want to make, but it's wise to plan them carefully to avoid overwhelming yourself. You need to balance this with your existing workload. Prioritise and look for quick wins with high impact and low effort.

34.1 Review your responses to each of the activities you've completed in your workbook and use them to make a list of the actions you need to take to improve your productivity.

34.2 Develop the actions into a plan with realistic timelines and success measures, making sure you prioritise those which will have the biggest impact. Don't do everything at once!

34.3 Celebrate! You have worked through a series of important questions about your personal and professional life, making a series of changes which will bring opportunities to grow and achieve even more. Give yourself a treat!

Activity 34: Your productivity action plan

Activity 34: Your productivity action plan

Activity 34: Your productivity action plan

Notes

Notes

Notes

Notes

Notes

Notes

Notes

Keep in touch

The best place to find out about my plans for other books in the School Financial Success Guides series is my website, at https://schoolfinancialsuccess.com. It's where you'll find my monthly blog and details of my books and online courses.

The first three books in the series are:

- School Budget Mastery: the basics and beyond

- Leading a School Budget Review

- Forecasting Your School's Funding

On the School Financial Success home page there's a red button which allows you to sign up for my free monthly newsletter. It contains a rundown of all the government announcements in the previous month relating to finance and funding in education and schools, with a brief explanation and links so you can read the original if you need more details. Why spend time trawling the web when I've done it for you? You'll also get to hear about my future plans and any speaking engagements or webinars that I've been asked to deliver.

Here are my links for social media platforms:

- My Facebook page can be found at: https://www.facebook.com/SchoolFinancialSuccess/. If you 'Like' the page, it will help it to be more visible in your feed.

- The Productivity for School Business Professionals page is at https://www.facebook.com/groups/ProductivitySBPs/.

- Twitter: https://twitter.com/juliecordiner

I hope you'll join the community discussions in any of these places.

Printed in Great Britain
by Amazon

45199166R00079